NATIONAL GEOGRAPHIC

T0308164

PASSPORT TO WONDER

PIONEER EDITION

By Marylou Tousignant

CONTENTS

2 Passport to Wonder

10 More Wonders

12 Concept Check

PASSPORT to WONDER

By Marylou Tousignant

What are the most amazing things ever built? Could you choose seven?

THAT'S WHAT the ancient Greeks did more than 2,000 years ago. Their list is called the Seven Wonders of the Ancient World.

Only one old wonder still stands today—the Pyramids of Giza. Nature and humans destroyed the others.

So a Swiss adventurer thought it was time for a new list. He held a contest. Millions of voters picked their favorites.

See the New 7 Wonders of the World yourself. Which do you like best?

Labor of Love

First stop: Agra, India.

You peer up at the Taj Mahal (left). It glows in the early morning light.

Yet this palace is really a tomb. It is a ruler's gift to his wife. Before dying, she asked for a **monument** to their love. The ruler spent more than 20 years building the Taj Mahal. It cost a fortune. Finally, in the 1650s, it was complete.

Today, the Taj Mahal still shines. Some people think it is the most beautiful building in the world. What do you think?

Winding Wall

Next stop: northern China.

You're on top of an enormous brick wall. It seems to stretch forever in both directions. This isn't just any wall. It's the Great Wall of China.

The Chinese began building walls more than 3,000 years ago. They built much of the Great Wall between 1368 and 1644. They wanted to keep enemies out.

Today, it is the world's largest human-made **structure.** It stretches more than 8,850 kilometers (almost 5,500 miles). That's twice the width of the United States!

Sand, storms, and earthquakes damage the wall. People take bricks from the wall. They use them as souvenirs or to build homes. You can help China save this treasure by taking only photos.

Monster Wall. *The Great Wall crosses northern China. It ends at a sea whose name means "Head of the Dragon."*

Seen on Screen. *Filmmakers set part of the movie* Indiana Jones and the Last Crusade *in Petra.*

Rock City

You've got one more stop in Asia: the country of Jordan.

You ride a camel through a canyon there. The pass is very narrow. Cliff walls rise above you. They look like city buildings. Are your eyes fooling you? No. You're standing in Petra.

About 2,000 years ago, people carved Petra out of rock cliffs. It was a busy city. Then an earthquake destroyed half of Petra. In time, people left. The city was forgotten.

In the 1800s, an explorer found Petra's **ruins**. Scientists have been digging out its treasures ever since. Watch where you step! Three-fourths of the city is still buried.

Easy Exit. *The Colosseum had 80 arched gates. Crowds could leave the huge stadium in about five minutes.*

Brutal Battles

Now you're off to Europe. Next stop: Rome, Italy.

You're facing a crumbling stadium. Huge chunks are missing. Fire and earthquakes have damaged it. Yet part still rises 48 meters (159 feet) in the air. It's the Roman Colosseum.

Close your eyes. Imagine a cheering crowd. When it opened in 80 C.E., the Colosseum was the place to go for fun. It held 50,000 people.

The people cheered as fighters called gladiators fought each other to the death. They also fought wild animals. Lions, bears, and even elephants sprang up from trap doors in the floor.

These brutal battles were outlawed in 523 C.E. The Colosseum closed soon after. Today, only tourists like you roam the arena.

Slithering Snakes

It's time to head to the Americas. Your first stop: Chichén Itzá, in southern Mexico.

The Maya and Toltec people lived here between the 7th and 13th centuries. They built amazing temples and pyramids. They also studied the stars. How talented were they? Take a look at the famous pyramid of Kukulkán. It is also known as *El Castillo*, or "The Castle."

Watch closely. Did you just see that snake-like shadow slither down its steps? The sun cast this shadow. The snake comes out on the first days of spring and fall. That's one way the people here kept track of time.

Yearly Steps. *The pyramid of Kukulkán has 91 steps on each side, plus one on top. That adds up to 365 steps. That's one step for each day of the year.*

Llama Land. *Llamas like the one in this photo live in the mountains around Machu Picchu. The city's name means "ancient mountain peak."*

Cloud City

Next stop: Peru.

How do you get to a city above the clouds? First, you hike through the Andes Mountains. The peaks here are steep! You wonder if you might slide right off.

Finally, you arrive at Machu Picchu. This city is sometimes called "the lost city of the Inca." The Inca were a rich and powerful people. They ruled the west part of South America.

No one is certain why or how the Inca built this city in such a rough landscape. Experts believe that it was a special place for Inca rulers. Check out the houses, temples, and tombs. Can you imagine some of these buildings covered in gold? They may have been!

Welcoming Arms

The end: Rio de Janeiro, Brazil. Take the train this time. It climbs Corcovado Mountain. The view from the top takes your breath away. The city spreads out below your feet. The Atlantic Ocean sparkles.

Look up. You see a huge statue. It weights 700 tons. It stands 38 meters (125 feet) tall. Its arms stretch 28 meters (92 feet) wide.

The people of Brazil gave the statue to themselves as a gift. It celebrated one hundred years of independence. Today, it's a symbol of Brazil's welcoming culture.

High Hike. *Visitors climb over 200 steps to reach the base of this giant statue.*

Wonder Why

It's time to go back home and wonder. Are the New 7 Wonders big enough? Are they beautiful enough?

There are many places that didn't make the list. Voters did not pick the Statue of Liberty. They skipped France's Eiffel Tower. No places in Africa or Australia won.

So think: What places would make your list? Then pack and go explore!

Entries/Entrées Visas Departures/Sorties Entries/Entrées

WORDWISE

monument: a famous place or building that celebrates a person, event, or idea

ruin: the remaining pieces of something

structure: a building or space that is made by people

14

MORE WONDERS

1. Crowning Touch.
A staircase leads to the Statue of Liberty's crown. The view? New York Harbor. It was once a stop for many immigrants to America.

2. Keeping Watch.
Why do giant statues guard Chile's Easter Island? Most have their backs to the sea. No one is sure why.

3. Ancient Wonder.
The largest pyramid ever built is near Giza, Egypt. Pharoh Khufu was buried here. So was a 4,600-year-old boat. It may be there to take him to his afterlife.

4. World Welcome.
The Eiffel Tower was built for the 1889 World's Fair in Paris, France. Critics called it "monstrous." Not anymore!

IN 2007, millions of people voted for the New 7 Wonders of the World. Fourteen finalists didn't make the cut. See if you recognize any of these runners-up.

8. Terrific Temple.
Angkor, Cambodia, is called "the city of temples." The most famous is Angkor Wat. Its tower is a symbol of a mythical mountain.

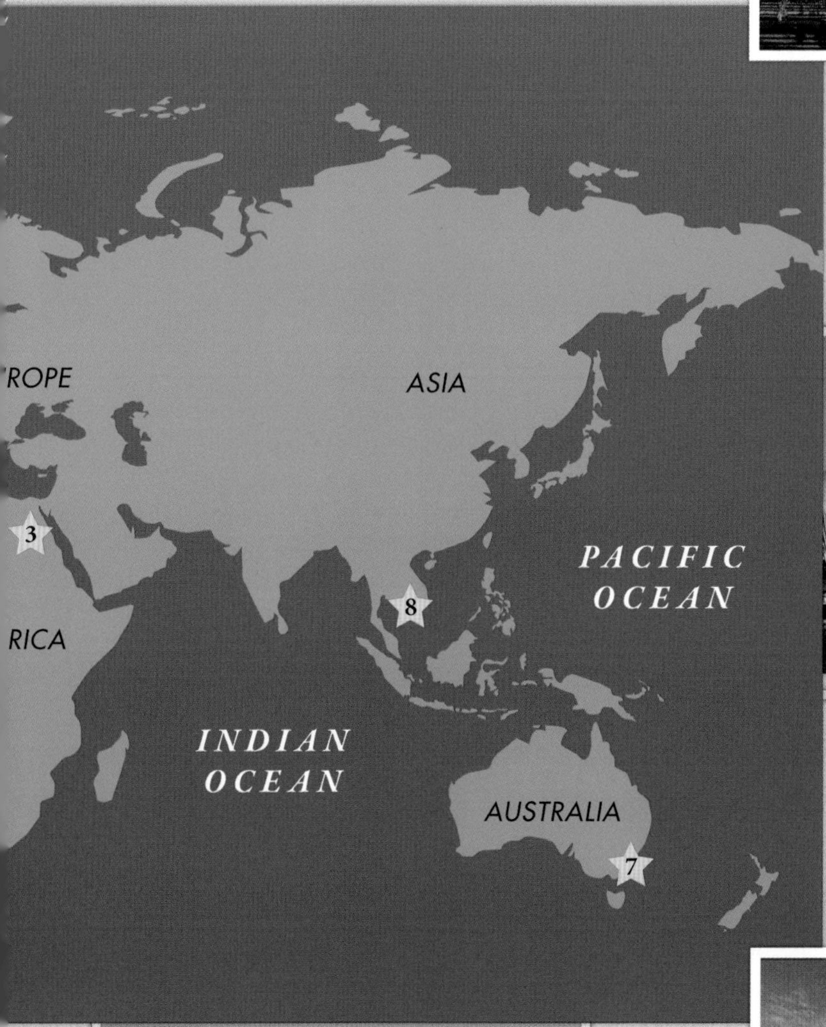

7. Sydney Sings.
How many tiles cover the Sydney Opera House in Australia? More than one million!

5. Fantastic Fort.
The name of Spain's Alhambra means "red fort" in Arabic. Yet inside, visitors find colorful tiles and fountains.

6. Desert Jewel.
Timbuktu was once called "the city of gold." Yet this African city's true treasure is knowledge. Thousands once studied at the mosque shown here.

WONDERFUL WORLD

Retrace your steps. Answer these questions about the New 7 Wonders of the World.

1. Why does the author call the Taj Mahal a "labor of love"?
2. What is surprising about the rock cliffs of Petra?
3. Name two of the Wonders found in the Americas.

4. Which of the runner-up Wonders is your favorite? Why?
5. Millions of people voted for the New Wonders. Why do you think the Wonders are important to so many people?